MUSHROOMS

MUSHROOMS

A BOOK OF RECIPES

HELEN SUDELL

LORENZ BOOKS

First published in 2013 by Lorenz Books
an imprint of Anness Publishing Limited
Blaby Road, Wigston, Leicestershire LE18 4SE
www.annesspublishing.com
www.lorenzbooks.com
info@anness.com

If you like the images in this book and would like to investigate
using them for publishing, promotions or advertising, please visit
our website www.practicalpictures.com for more information

A CIP catalogue record for this book is available from
The British Library

Publisher Joanna Lorenz
Editorial Director Helen Sudell
Designer Nigel Partridge
Illustrations Anna Koska

Photographers: Martin Brigdale, Nicki Dowey, William Lingwood,
    Craig Robertson, Jon Whitaker, Gus Filgate, Will Heap,
    Charlie Richards
Recipes by: Ghillie Basan, Jenny White, Joanna Farrow, Pepita Aris,
    Ewa Michalik, Jeni Wright, Annette Yates, Christine Ingram,
    Carol Pastor, Miguel de Castro e Silva, Elena Makhonko,
    Valentina Harris, Janez Bogataj

Printed and bound in China

COOK'S NOTES

• Bracketed terms are intended for American readers.

• For all recipes, quantities are given in both metric and imperial
measures and, where appropriate, in standard cups and spoons.
Follow one set of measures, but not a mixture, because they are
not interchangeable.

• Standard spoon and cup measures are level. 1 tsp = 5ml, 1 tbsp =
15ml, 1 cup = 250ml/8fl oz.

• Australian standard tablespoons are 20ml. Australian readers
should use 3 tsp in place of 1 tbsp for measuring small quantities.

• American pints are 16fl oz/2 cups. American readers should use
20fl oz/2.5 cups in place of 1 pint when measuring liquids.

• Electric oven temperatures in this book are for conventional
ovens. When using a fan oven, the temperature will probably need
to be reduced by about 10–20°C/20–40°F. Since ovens vary, you
should check with your manufacturer's instruction book for
guidance.

• The nutritional analysis given for each recipe is calculated per
portion (i.e. serving or item), unless otherwise stated. If the recipe
gives a range, such as Serves 4–6, then the nutritional analysis will
be for the smaller portion size, i.e. 6 servings. The analysis does not
include optional ingredients, such as salt added to taste.

• Medium (US large) eggs are used unless otherwise stated.

PUBLISHER'S NOTE

CONTENTS

INTRODUCTION

Mushrooms are one of the most mysterious of food stuffs, literally springing up overnight ready to be plucked and cooked within hours. In recent years wild mushrooms and a wide variety of cultivated mushrooms have become readily available and we can now celebrate this fabulously versatile vegetable. The meaty texture of many types of mushrooms means they make excellent additions to stews, casseroles or sauces. Their affinity with both butter

Below: Button (white) mushrooms are available all year round.

and olive oil allows them to be often cooked very simply and served alone, perhaps with a sprinkling of fresh parsley.

Most people associate mushrooms with the autumn, but, in fact, they can be found growing in the wild throughout the year. The spring brings morels and the St George's mushroom. The first of the summer crop is usually the field mushroom before the large autumn harvest of ceps, portobello, chestnut and shiitake comes to the fore. Even in the winter, on mild days, you can find oyster mushrooms growing happily in the forest.

PICKING MUSHROOMS

Going out into the local fields and woodland to pick your own mushrooms is a wonderful experience. It is important to be sure you can properly identify the mushrooms you pick as many mushrooms are poisonous, but as long as you

Above: The light brown oyster mushroom will continue to grow late into the autumn.

have a good field guide and are sensible, picking and then cooking your own mushrooms can be a lot of fun. Mushrooms grow almost exclusively during the hours of darkness. As a result, the best specimens are picked when they are fresh in the early morning. The equipment you will need is very simple: a small field guide for identification purposes, a sharp knife and brush (to remove the obvious dirt), a light open-weave basket, several plastic bags or disposable gloves to handle specimens about which you are doubtful, and finally, a good strong stick. The stick will be used to part ferns and undergrowth to see if any mushrooms are hidden there. You can also use it to turn over any specimens you may not wish to touch until you have properly identified them. If in doubt about the identity of a mushroom do not collect it and never, ever, eat anything you cannot identify with certainty.

BUYING AND STORING MUSHROOMS

Choose mushrooms that are firm and moist but without damp patches or dry tail ends. Some wild mushroom varieties may have worms; these are not harmful and can be cut away before cooking. To establish if any are present, break off the stems of a few and cut through the caps.

Mushrooms do not store well if they become wet or sweaty.

Store them in a refrigerator in a paper bag or covered with a damp cloth. They keep for up to four days in this way.

Dried mushrooms keep indefinitely in an airtight container in a cool place. Before use, soak them in tepid water for 25–30 minutes.

COOKING MUSHROOMS

Nutritionally, mushrooms contain very little but fibre and protein. They are valued for their strong, distinctive flavour and particular chewy texture

Above: To pick mushrooms at their best, it is better to go hunting early in the morning.

when cooked. Only cultivated mushrooms can be eaten raw with safety. All other wild mushrooms should always be cooked. Because they produce a lot of liquid and shrink in size, mushrooms are best cooked by first sautéeing them in butter or olive oil, which seals in their flavour. Use the soaking liquid from dried mushrooms to add interest to sauces and stocks.

TYPES OF MUSHROOM

Mushrooms come in all shapes and sizes and all have distinct qualities and uses.

BUTTON (WHITE)
The flavour is very mild, and they are good sliced and eaten raw in salads.

CANNED BUTTON
These make a useful addition to soups, stews, pasta and rice dishes.

CLOSED CUP
These tend to have a mild taste and are good eaten raw or lightly cooked in stir-fries.

OPEN CUP
At this stage the brown gills are showing and the cap is darker. Good for stuffing and baking.

FIELD (PORTOBELLO)
When the cap is quite flat, mushrooms have the best flavour and are ideal in soups or fried with bacon for breakfast.

SHIITAKE
These are of Asian origin and are moist and fleshy with a strong flavour.

MORELS
These are intensely perfumed, expensive and beloved of gourmets. Morels are available dried from delicatessens.

OYSTER
Moist, delicate pale grey or yellow flesh, they are so named because they are thought to resemble oyster shells.

Below: Dried wild mushrooms have an intense, earthy flavour.

BOLETUS, CEP OR PORCINI
The boletus has a round brown cap and thick stem. It is strong in flavour, and is often dried.

CHANTERELLE (GIROLLE)
These are very versatile, tasting exquisite whether on their own, or with meat or fish. They give an elegant colour to sauces.

CHESTNUT (CREMINI)
All-purpose mushrooms with brown caps, also known as champignons de Paris.

CLOUD EAR (WOOD EAR)
Mainly sold dried. As they are quite gelatinous in texture it is important to cook them well.

TRUMPET
Often used in Japanese cooking, they have a long shelf life.

PRESERVED MUSHROOMS
Wild varieties are frequently preserved in oil and sometimes roasted over charcoal first.

Preserved mushrooms

Sliced button mushrooms

Small chestnut mushrooms

Open cup mushrooms

Yellow oyster mushrooms

Button mushrooms

Shiitake mushrooms

Closed cup mushrooms

Dried ceps

Canned button mushrooms

Dried morels

Field mushrooms

Oyster mushrooms

Preserved mushrooms

Chestnut mushrooms

BASIC TECHNIQUES AND RECIPES

Both cultivated and wild mushrooms will have some soil or sand clinging to them and they must be cleaned properly before cooking.

PREPARING MUSHROOMS

Mushrooms absorb water easily and must not be allowed to become waterlogged, however those with deep gills or pockets, such as morels, can be soaked for a few minutes to remove any grit.

Trim the stem ends from wild mushrooms only if they are bruised. Small mushrooms can be left whole; larger ones can be sliced or chopped. Rinse or wipe mushrooms with a damp cloth or kitchen paper.

DRYING MUSHROOMS

Mushrooms can be dried easily. Dried mushrooms will keep in a sterilized, airtight jar for many months and can be added to soups and stews.

Wipe the mushrooms with a damp cloth and slice the mushrooms thinly. Arrange the slices in a single layer on a basket tray or baking sheet lined with non-stick baking parchment. Put the tray in a warm, airy place for a few days until they are completely dry. Place the dried mushrooms in an air-tight, sterilized jar, label and store in a dark place. If the mushrooms are not completely dry, moulds may develop in storage. Check before using.

FREEZING MUSHROOMS

Mushrooms can be frozen successfully as they retain their flavour when thawed. Firmer varieties such as shiitake, closed cup and flat mushrooms are suitable candidates for freezing. Thaw them by dropping them briefly into boiling water just before use.

Ensure the mushrooms are clean and free from grit and insects. Slice them thickly if they are large. Drop them into a pan of boiling salted water for 1 minute. Remove and drain well. Open freeze on a tray for 30–40 minutes. Store them in plastic bags or rigid containers in the freezer. They will keep for up to six months.

MARINATED MUSHROOMS
Makes 1 litre/1¾ pints/4 cups
500g/1¼lb/8 cups wild
   mushrooms
500ml/17fl oz/2 cups water
25ml/1½ tbsp salt
30ml/2 tbsp white wine vinegar
15–30ml/1–2 tbsp sugar
5–6 allspice berries
5–6 cloves
2 bay leaves
1 garlic clove
2–3 stems fresh dill

Wipe the mushrooms with a damp cloth or kitchen paper to remove any dirt. Cut large mushrooms in half but leave the small ones whole.

Put the mushrooms in a large pan, add the water and 15ml/ 1 tbsp salt. Bring to the boil, then reduce the heat and simmer for about 30 minutes, stirring occasionally.

Add the remaining salt, the vinegar, sugar, allspice, cloves, bay leaves, and whole garlic clove to the mushrooms. Simmer for a further 10 minutes. Set aside until completely cool.

Put the dill in the bottom of clean, sterilized glass jars. Pour in the spiced mushrooms with the marinade and seal tightly.

Store in the refrigerator and use within 2 months.

MUSHROOM SAUCE
Makes 150ml/¼ pint/¾ cup
mushrooms and salt (see below)
For the spice mix
3 garlic cloves, chopped
2 red chillies, chopped
5ml/1 tsp ground allspice
2.5ml/½ tsp grated nutmeg
2.5ml/½ tsp ground ginger
300ml/½ pint/1¼ cups red wine

You will need 15ml/1 tbsp salt for every 450g/1lb mushrooms used. Chop the mushrooms and

place in an ovenproof pan (tin), sprinkling the salt over. Leave, covered in clear film (plastic wrap), for 3 days to exude the juices. Press occasionally.

Preheat the oven to 110°C/225°F/Gas 2. Heat the pan of mushrooms for 3 hours to remove all moisture.

Strain the mushrooms. Measure the quantity of strained mushroom liquid: for every 1 litre/1¾ pints/4 cups of liquid, allow one batch of the spice mix including the wine.

Add the spices and wine to the mushroom liquid and bring to the boil. Return to the oven for 2–3 hours. Strain the sauce and pour into warmed sterilized jars or bottles. Use as required to flavour sauces and stews.

SOUPS AND APPETIZERS

MUSHROOMS ADD SCENTED FLAVOUR TO SOUPS
AND SIMPLE SNACKS SUCH AS MUSHROOMS ON
HOT BUTTERED TOAST. THEY ALSO MAKE TASTY
VEGETARIAN BLINIS AND, COMBINED WITH
SCALLOPS, CREATE A SPLENDID STARTER

TORTELLINI CHANTERELLE BROTH

The savoury, sweet quality of chanterelle mushrooms combines well in a simple broth with spinach and ricotta tortellini. The sherry adds a lovely warming effect.

Serves 4

350g/12oz fresh spinach and ricotta tortellini, or 175g/6oz dried

1.2 litres/2 pints/5 cups chicken stock

75ml/5 tbsp dry sherry

175g/6oz/2 cups fresh chanterelle (girolle) mushrooms, trimmed and sliced, or 15g/½oz/½ cup dried chanterelles

chopped fresh parsley, to garnish

Energy 204kcal/859kJ; Protein 7.6g; Carbohydrate 23.4g, of which sugars 1.5g; Fat 4.3g, of which saturates 0.1g; Cholesterol 0mg; Calcium 106mg; Fibre 1.6g; Sodium 185mg.

Cook the tortellini according to the packet instructions. Bring the chicken stock to the boil, add the dry sherry and fresh or dried mushrooms and then simmer for 10 minutes.

Strain the tortellini, add to the stock, then ladle the broth into four warmed bowls, making sure each contains the same proportions of tortellini and mushrooms. Garnish with the chopped parsley and serve in warmed soup bowls.

MUSHROOM AND TARRAGON SOUP

This delightful mix of ingredients sees the earthy flavours of the mushrooms combine with the sour cream and fresh tarragon to produce a satisfying and warming appetizer or main meal.

Serves 6

300g/11oz/4 cups field
    (portobello) mushrooms
30ml/2 tbsp olive oil
2 shallots, finely chopped
600ml/1 pint/2½ cups
    vegetable stock
30ml/2 tbsp fresh tarragon,
    chopped, plus extra to
    garnish
45ml/3 tbsp sour cream
salt and ground black pepper
slices of wholegrain bread,
    to serve

COOK'S TIP
When sautéeing the
mushrooms use a large
pan to maximize the
cooking heat.

Clean and slice the mushrooms quite finely.

Add the olive oil to a large pan and heat gently. Add the shallots, sauté for 2–3 minutes and add the mushrooms. Sauté for 5 minutes.

Add the stock and season. Simmer for 15–20 minutes, covered. When the soup has thickened, add the chopped tarragon and remove the soup from the heat.

Add the sour cream and mix to combine, while the soup is still hot. Serve, garnished with tarragon, and accompanied with crusty bread.

329kcal/1356kJ; Protein 1g; Carbohydrate 5g, of which sugars 15g; Fat 35g, of which saturates 6g; Cholesterol 5mg; Calcium 15mg; Fibre 1.3g; Sodium 268mg.

BARLEY AND MUSHROOM SOUP

This recipe originates from Latvia, where barley and mushrooms are two of the most common ingredients to be found in the Latvian kitchen. They combine perfectly in this rich, satisfying soup.

Serves 6

150g/5oz/generous ½ cup pearl
    barley
45ml/3 tbsp vegetable oil
1 onion, thinly sliced
400g/14oz/5½ cups
    mushrooms, thinly sliced
45ml/3 tbsp lemon juice
1 litre/1¾ pints/4 cups
    vegetable stock
200ml/7fl oz/scant 1 cup sour
    cream
45ml/3 tbsp dill, finely chopped
salt and ground black pepper
2 hard-boiled eggs, finely
    chopped

Put the barley in a large bowl and cover with cold water. Soak overnight in a cool place, then rinse with cold water and drain. Heat the oil in a large, heavy pan and cook the onion for 5 minutes, or until softened but not browned.

Add the mushrooms and cook for a further 10 minutes. Add the lemon juice and barley, and stir well. Pour in the stock, then bring to the boil. Simmer for 45 minutes, or until the barley is cooked and soft. Season to taste, then leave to cool.

Stir in the sour cream and dill, reserving a little dill to garnish. Chill the soup, then ladle the cold soup into bowls and serve, garnished with the chopped eggs and dill.

Energy 247kcal/1033kJ; Protein 6.6g; Carbohydrate 23.4g, of which sugars 2.1g; Fat 14.9g, of which saturates 5.3g; Cholesterol 83mg; Calcium 67mg; Fibre 1.3g; Sodium 44mg.

MUSHROOMS ON TOAST

Cultivated or wild mushrooms make a delicious addition to a full English breakfast. They also make a meaty treat when cooked with cream and served on toast.

Serves 2
250g/9oz/3 cups button (white) or closed-cup mushrooms
5ml/1 tsp olive oil
15g/½oz butter, plus extra for spreading
60ml/4 tbsp double (heavy) cream
freshly grated nutmeg
2 thick slices of bread
chopped chives or parsley, to garnish
salt and ground black pepper

Energy 350kcal/1460kJ; Protein 6.8g; Carbohydrate 25.7g, of which sugars 2.1g; Fat 25.3g, of which saturates 14.2g; Cholesterol 57mg; Calcium 78mg; Fibre 2g; Sodium 318mg.

Pick over and trim the mushrooms and cut into thick slices.

Heat the oil and butter in a non-stick pan, add the sliced mushrooms and cook quickly for about 3 minutes, stirring frequently.

Stir in the cream and season with salt, pepper and a little nutmeg. Simmer for 1–2 minutes.

Toast the bread and spread with butter. Top with the mushrooms, sprinkle with chopped herbs and serve.

MUSHROOM PICKER'S OMELETTE

Enthusiastic mushroom pickers have been known to carry with them a portable gas stove, an omelette pan and a few eggs, ready to assemble an on-site brunch.

Serves 1

25 g/1 oz/2 tbsp unsalted butter, plus extra for cooking
115 g/4 oz/1¼ cups assorted wild and cultivated mushrooms, trimmed and sliced
3 eggs, at room temperature
salt and ground black pepper
crusty bread and salad, to serve
chopped parsley, to garnish

Melt the butter in a small omelette pan, add the mushrooms and cook until the juices run. Season, remove from pan and set aside. Wipe the pan.

Break the eggs into a bowl, season and beat with a fork. Heat the omelette pan over a high heat, add a knob (pat) of butter and let it begin to brown. Pour in the beaten egg and stir briskly with the back of a fork.

When the eggs are two-thirds scrambled, add the mushrooms and let the omelette finish cooking for just 10–15 seconds.

Tap the handle of the omelette pan sharply with your fist to loosen the omelette from the pan, then fold and turn on to a plate. Garnish with parsley and serve with crusty bread and a simple green salad.

COOK'S TIPS

• From start to finish, an omelette should be cooked and on the table in less than a minute.
• For best results, use free-range (farm-fresh) eggs at room temperature.

Energy 216Kcal/898kJ; Protein 13g; Carbohydrate 2g, of which sugars 1g; Fat 11g, of which saturates 4g; Cholesterol 349mg; Calcium 87mg; Fibre 4.3g; Sodium 400mg.

CARAMELIZED MUSHROOMS WITH ALLSPICE AND HERBS

Button (white) mushrooms caramelize beautifully in their own juice, but still keep their moistness and nutty flavour. They are delicious served on toasted crusty bread as a light appetizer.

Serves 4

45ml/3 tbsp olive oil
15ml/1 tbsp butter
450g/1lb/5 cups button (white) mushrooms, wiped clean
3–4 garlic cloves, finely chopped
10ml/2 tsp allspice berries, crushed
10ml/2 tsp coriander seeds
5ml/1 tsp dried mint
1 bunch each of fresh sage and flat leaf parsley, chopped
salt and ground black pepper
toasted crusty bread and lemon wedges, to serve

Energy 125kcal/517kJ; Protein 2.8g;
Carbohydrate 1.2g, of which sugars 0.8g;
Fat 12.2g, of which saturates 3.3g;
Cholesterol 8mg; Calcium 58mg; Fibre
2.5g; Sodium 37mg.

Heat the oil and butter in a wide, heavy pan, then stir in the mushrooms with the garlic, allspice and coriander seeds. Cover and cook for about 10 minutes, shaking the pan from time to time, until the mushrooms start to caramelize.

Remove the lid and toss in the mint with some of the sage and parsley. Cook for a further 5 minutes, until most of the liquid has evaporated, then season with salt and pepper.

Tip the mushrooms into a serving dish and sprinkle the rest of the sage and parsley over the top. Serve hot or at room temperature, with lemon wedges for squeezing.

BUCKWHEAT BLINIS WITH MUSHROOM CAVIAR

These little Russian pancakes are traditionally served with fish roe caviar and sour cream. Here is a vegetarian alternative that uses a selection of wild mushrooms in place of fish roe.

Serves 4

115g/4oz/1 cup strong white
    bread flour
50g/2oz/½ cup buckwheat
    flour
2.5ml/½ tsp salt
300ml/½ pint/1¼ cups milk
5ml/1 tsp dried yeast
2 eggs, separated
200ml/7fl oz/1 cup sour cream

For the caviar

350g/12oz/4 cups mixed wild
    mushrooms, chopped
5ml/1 tsp celery salt
30ml/2 tbsp walnut oil
15ml/1 tbsp lemon juice
45ml/3 tbsp chopped fresh
    parsley, plus extra to garnish
ground black pepper
paprika, to garnish

Energy 380kcal/1586kJ; Protein 12.5g;
Carbohydrate 38.8g, of which sugars 6.2g;
Fat 20.6g, of which saturates 8.5g;
Cholesterol 130mg; Calcium 205mg; Fibre
2.3g; Sodium 94mg.

To make the caviar, place the mushrooms in a glass bowl, toss with the salt and cover with a weighted plate. Leave for 2 hours until the juices have run out into the base of the bowl. Rinse to remove the salt, drain and press out as much liquid as you can. Return the mushrooms to the bowl and toss with walnut oil, lemon juice, parsley and pepper. Chill.

Sift the two flours together with the salt in a mixing bowl. Gently warm the milk then add the yeast, stirring until dissolved. Pour into the flour, add the egg yolks and stir to make a smooth batter. Cover with a clean damp dish towel and leave in a warm place for 1 hour.

Whisk the egg whites in a clean grease-free bowl until stiff then fold into the risen batter. Heat a griddle pan, moisten with oil, then drop spoonfuls of the batter onto the surface. When bubbles rise to the top, turn them over and cook briefly on the other side. Spoon on the sour cream, top with the caviar, sprinkle parsley and paprika over, and serve.

DEEP-FRIED LAYERED SHIITAKE AND SCALLOPS

In this dish, you can taste three kinds of softness: chewy shiitake, mashed naga-imo with miso, and succulent scallop. The mixture creates a moment of heaven in your mouth.

Serves 4

4 scallops
8 large fresh shiitake mushrooms
225g/8oz naga-imo, unpeeled
20ml/4 tsp miso
50g/2oz/1 cup fresh
　breadcrumbs
cornflour (cornstarch), for
　dusting
vegetable oil, for deep-frying
2 eggs, beaten
salt
4 lemon wedges, to serve

COOK'S TIP

If you can't find naga-imo,
use yam or 115g/4oz each
of peeled potatoes and
Jerusalem artichokes
instead. Cook the potatoes
and the artichokes until
both are tender.

Energy 221kcal/918kJ; Protein 11.2g;
Carbohydrate 11.7g, of which sugars 1.5g;
Fat 14.6g, of which saturates 2.3g;
Cholesterol 107mg; Calcium 50mg; Fibre
1.1g; Sodium 183mg.

Slice the scallops in two horizontally, then sprinkle with salt. Remove the stalks from the shiitake.

Cut shallow slits on the top of the shiitake to form a "hash" symbol or cut slits to form a white cross. Sprinkle with a little salt.

Heat a steamer and steam the naga-imo for 10–15 minutes, or until soft. Test with a skewer. Leave to cool.

Wait until the naga-imo is cool enough to handle. Skin, then mash the flesh in a bowl with a masher, getting rid of any lumps. Add the miso and mix well. Take the breadcrumbs into your hands and break them down finely. Mix half into the mashed naga-imo, keeping the rest on a small plate.

Fill the underneath of the shiitake caps with a scoop of mashed naga-imo. Smooth down with the flat edge of a knife and dust the mash with cornflour.

Add a little mash to a slice of scallop and place on top.

Spread another 5ml/1 tsp mashed naga-imo on to the scallop and shape to completely cover. Make sure all the ingredients are clinging together. Repeat to make eight little mounds.

Heat the oil to 150°C/300°F. Place the beaten eggs in a shallow container. Dust the shiitake and scallop mounds with cornflour, then dip into the egg. Handle with care as the mash and scallop are quite soft. Coat well with the remaining breadcrumbs and deep-fry in the oil until golden. Drain well on kitchen paper. Serve hot on individual plates with a wedge of lemon.

WILD MUSHROOM AND PINE NUT MUFFINS

These lightly flavoured savoury muffins make attractive accompaniments to soft cheeses, pâtés and soups. The pine nuts add texture and crunch, and a warm nutty flavour.

Makes 6–7 large muffins

250g/9oz/2¼ cups self-raising
  (self-rising) flour
11.5ml/2¼ tsp baking powder
150g/5oz/1¾ cups mixture of
  wild mushrooms
90g/3½oz/scant ½ cup butter,
  for frying
large pinch cayenne pepper
large pinch mace
50–75g/2–3oz/½–¾ cup
  pine nuts
30ml/2 tbsp olive oil
90ml/6 tbsp buttermilk
75g/3oz/6 tbsp butter, melted
2 eggs

Preheat the oven to 180°C/350°F/Gas 4. Lightly grease the cups of a muffin tin (pan). In a large bowl, sift the flour and baking powder and set aside.

Clean and slice the mushrooms. In a frying pan, heat 75g/3oz/6 tbsp of the butter over a medium heat. When it is foaming, add the mushrooms. Season with cayenne pepper and mace. Fry gently, stirring, until just softened. Scrape into a bowl and set aside to cool.

Fry the pine nuts in the remaining butter and the olive oil for 30 seconds. Add to the mushrooms.

Beat together the buttermilk, melted butter and eggs in a bowl. Stir into the dry ingredients with the mushrooms and pine nuts.

Spoon the batter into the muffin tins and bake for 25 minutes until the tops are golden and firm.

Energy 399kcal/1660kJ; Protein 6.9g;
Carbohydrate 28g, of which sugars 1.4g;
Fat 29.6g, of which saturates 14.2g;
Cholesterol 109mg; Calcium 154mg; Fibre
1.5g; Sodium 334mg.

VEGETARIAN
MEALS

A VARIETY OF WILD AND CULTIVATED

MUSHROOMS DEMONSTRATE THEIR AMAZING

VERSATILITY IN A DIVERSE ARRAY OF RECIPES,

FROM BEAN DISHES TO SAVOURY FRITTERS, AND

FROM SPICY SAUTÉES TO CRISP PASTRIES

LENTILS WITH MUSHROOMS AND ANIS

In Spain, the great plains of Castile produce lentils for the whole of Europe. Locally they are weekly fare. In this recipe they are flavoured with another product of the region, anis spirit.

Serves 4

30ml/2 tbsp olive oil
1 large onion, sliced
2 garlic cloves, finely chopped
250g/9oz/3 cups chestnut
  (cremini) mushrooms, sliced
150g/5oz/generous ½ cup
  brown or green lentils,
  soaked overnight
4 tomatoes, cut in eighths
1 bay leaf
25g/1oz/½ cup chopped
  fresh parsley
30ml/2 tbsp anis spirit
  or anisette
salt, paprika and black pepper

COOK'S TIP
If you forget to soak the lentils overnight, add at least 30 minutes to the cooking time.

Heat the oil in a flameproof casserole. Add the onion and fry gently, with the garlic, until softened but not browned.

Add the sliced mushrooms and stir to combine with the onion and garlic. Continue cooking, stirring gently, for a couple of minutes.

Add the lentils, tomatoes and bay leaf with 175ml/6fl oz/¾ cup water. Simmer gently, covered, for 30–40 minutes until the lentils are soft, and the liquid has almost disappeared.

Stir in the parsley and anis. Season with salt, paprika and black pepper.

Energy 242kcal/1018kJ; Protein 12.5g; Carbohydrate 29.8g, of which sugars 9.5g; Fat 7.2g, of which saturates 1g; Cholesterol 0mg; Calcium 83mg; Fibre 6.9g; Sodium 23mg.

PAN-FRIED CHILLI PARSNIP AND SHIITAKE MUSHROOMS

The traditional version of this dish has its roots in the temples of Korea, although the contemporary version given here adds more spices and seasoning than the original.

Serves 4

150g/5oz parsnips, finely sliced
sesame oil, to season
vegetable oil, for frying
115g/4oz/1¼ cups fresh
    shiitake mushrooms
salt
15ml/1 tbsp pine nuts, ground,
    to garnish

For the sauce

45ml/3 tbsp chilli paste
5ml/1 tsp chilli powder
15ml/1 tbsp maple syrup
5ml/1 tsp sugar
5ml/1 tsp soy sauce
5ml/1 tsp sesame oil

Place the parsnips in a bowl and add a little sesame oil and salt. Coat the slices evenly. Set aside for 10 minutes.

For the sauce, mix the chilli paste and powder, maple syrup, sugar, soy sauce and sesame oil with a little water.

Heat a frying pan and add a little vegetable oil. Sauté the finely sliced parsnips until they are softened and lightly browned. Then transfer the parsnips to a bowl and coat them with chilli sauce.

Discard the stalks from the shiitake mushrooms and spoon the remaining chilli sauce into the caps.

Return the sautéed parsnips to the pan, with their sauce, and then add the mushrooms. Cook the parsnip and mushroom mixture over low heat. When the vegetables are cooked and the liquid has reduced, serve, seasoned with sesame oil and a sprinkling of ground pine nuts.

Energy 86kcal/362kJ; Protein 2.3g;
Carbohydrate 10.4g, of which sugars 6.4g;
Fat 4.4g, of which saturates 0.5g;
Cholesterol 0mg; Calcium 26mg; Fibre
2.1g; Sodium 106mg.

MUSHROOM POLENTA

This simple recipe uses freshly made polenta, but for an even easier version you can substitute ready made polenta and slice it straight into the dish, ready for baking.

Serves 4
1 litre/1³⁄₄ pints/4 cups water
5ml/1 tsp salt
250g/9oz/1½ cups quick-cook polenta
50g/2oz/¼ cup butter
400g/14oz/5 cups chestnut (cremini) mushrooms, sliced
175g/6oz/1½ cups grated Gruyère cheese
ground black pepper

Energy 518kcal/2155kJ; Protein 18.9g; Carbohydrate 46.2g, of which sugars 0.3g; Fat 27.2g, of which saturates 16.1g; Cholesterol 69mg; Calcium 334mg; Fibre 2.5g; Sodium 397mg.

Line a 28 x 18cm/11 x 7in shallow baking tin (pan) with baking parchment. Bring the water and salt to the boil in a large pan. Add the polenta in a steady stream, stirring constantly. Bring back to the boil, stirring, and cook for 5 minutes, until thick and smooth. Turn the polenta into the prepared tin and spread it out into an even layer. Leave to cool.

Preheat the oven to 200°C/400°F/Gas 6. Melt the butter in a frying pan and cook the mushrooms for 3–5 minutes, until golden. Season with salt and lots of freshly ground black pepper.

Turn out the polenta on to a chopping board. Peel away the parchment and cut the polenta into large squares. Pile the squares into a shallow, ovenproof dish. Sprinkle with half the cheese, then pile the mushrooms on top and pour over their buttery juices. Sprinkle with the remaining cheese and bake for about 20 minutes.

LEMON, THYME AND ADUKI STUFFED MUSHROOMS

Field mushrooms have a rich flavour and a meaty texture that go well with this fragrant herb and lemon stuffing. The aduki beans are high in protein and fibre but low in fat.

Serves 4–6

200g/7oz/1 cup dried or 400g/14oz/2 cups drained, canned aduki beans
45ml/3 tbsp olive oil, plus extra for brushing
1 onion, finely chopped
2 garlic cloves, crushed
30ml/2 tbsp fresh chopped or 5ml/1 tsp dried thyme
8 large field (portobello) mushrooms, stalks finely chopped
50g/2oz/1 cup fresh wholemeal (whole-wheat) breadcrumbs
juice of 1 lemon
185g/6½oz/¾ cup goat's cheese, crumbled
salt and freshly ground black pepper
spinach leaves, to serve

If using dried beans, soak them overnight, then drain and rinse well. Place in a pan, add enough water to cover and bring to the boil. Continue to boil rapidly for 10 minutes, then reduce the heat, cook for 30 minutes until tender, then drain. If using canned beans, rinse, drain well, then set aside.

Preheat the oven to 200°C/400°F/Gas 6. Heat the oil in a large, heavy frying pan, add the onion and garlic and sauté for 5 minutes until softened. Add the thyme and the mushroom stalks and cook for a further 3 minutes, stirring occasionally, until tender.

Stir in the beans, breadcrumbs and lemon juice, season well, then cook for 2 minutes until heated through. Mash two-thirds of the beans with a fork or potato masher, leaving the remaining beans whole.

Brush a baking dish and the base and sides of the mushrooms with oil, then top each one with a spoonful of the bean mixture. Place the mushrooms in the dish, cover with foil and bake for 20 minutes. Remove the foil. Top each mushroom with some of the goat's cheese and bake for a further 15 minutes, or until the cheese is melted and bubbly and the mushrooms are tender.

Serve with steamed spinach leaves.

Energy 430kcal/1795kJ; Protein 16g; Carbohydrate 29g, of which sugars 5g; Fat 28g, of which saturates 7g; Cholesterol 24mg; Calcium 211mg; Fibre 2g; Sodium 547mg.

MUSHROOM AND QUAIL'S EGGS GOUGÈRE

Traditionally, these little pastry buns are topped with Gruyère cheese and served with a glass of wine. Here the gougère is filled with wild mushrooms and tiny, lightly boiled quail's eggs.

Serves 4–6

75ml/3oz/6 tbsp butter, cut into
    small pieces
2.5ml/½ tsp salt
175ml/6fl oz/¾ cup water
100g/3¾oz/scant 1 cup plain
    (all-purpose) flour, sifted
4 eggs
115g/4oz/1 cup Gruyère
    cheese, grated
25g/1oz/2 tbsp butter
1 onion, chopped
2 celery sticks, sliced
350g/12oz/4 cups mixed wild
    mushrooms, halved or
    quartered
25g/1oz/¼ cup cornflour
    (cornstarch)
150ml/¼ pint/⅔ cup red wine
    and water, mixed
150ml/¼ pint/⅔ cup stock
15ml/1 tbsp chopped flat leaf
    parsley
12 quail's eggs

Preheat the oven to 220°F/425°F/Gas 7. In a saucepan, melt the butter with the salt and water, and bring to the boil. Remove from the heat, add the flour all at once and beat hard with a wooden spoon until it forms a ball.

Return the pan to the heat and cook, beating hard, for 1–2 minutes. Leave to cool slightly. Add two of the eggs, beating until the mixture becomes smooth and glossy. Beat in the third egg until smooth, then beat in as much of the fourth egg as you need to attain a smooth, glossy, soft, dropping consistency. Beat in half of the Gruyère cheese.

Place a round of non-stick baking paper on a baking tray and place large spoonfuls of the mixture evenly in a circle about 20cm/8in. Place them close together so that they will join up while they cook. Bake for about 35 minutes until well risen and golden all over. Remove from the oven and set aside to cool slightly.

Meanwhile, heat the butter in a saucepan, and fry the onion and celery until softened. Add the mushrooms and cook gently until their juices run. Blend together the cornflour and wine. Add the stock to the mushrooms and gradually stir in the cornflour mixture. Cook gently until thickened. Add the parsley and cook gently for a few minutes until quite thick.

Place the quail's eggs in a pan of cold water, bring to the boil and cook for 1 minute. Cool thoroughly, then peel.

To serve, slice the gougère in half horizontally. Fill with the mushrooms and top with the eggs. Replace the top, sprinkle over the remaining cheese and return to the oven until the cheese melts.

Energy 364kcal/1513kJ; Protein 14.7g; Carbohydrate 17.4g, of which sugars 4.5g; Fat 26.1g, of which saturates 14.1g; Cholesterol 150mg; Calcium 283mg; Fibre 2.4g; Sodium 327mg.

FRIED MUSHROOMS WITH ROOT VEGETABLES

This is a wonderful way to use up a glut of fresh mushrooms to make a tasty, hearty meal. The mushrooms bring earthy flavour while the root vegetables provide substance.

Serves 4

350g/12oz/4 cups fresh mushrooms, such as porcini, cut into small pieces
65g/2½oz/5 tbsp butter
2 onions, peeled and chopped
1 turnip, finely diced
3 carrots, finely diced
3–4 potatoes, finely diced
60–75ml/4–5 tbsp finely chopped fresh parsley
100ml/3½fl oz/scant ½ cup smetana or crème fraîche
salt and ground black pepper

Heat a large frying pan, add the mushrooms and cook over a medium heat, stirring frequently, until all liquid has evaporated. Add half of the butter and the onions and stir-fry for 10 minutes.

In a separate frying pan, heat the remaining butter until melted. Add the turnip, carrots and potatoes, in two or three batches, and fry for 10–15 minutes, until softened and golden brown.

Mix the mushrooms and the fried root vegetables together, cover the pan and cook for about 10 minutes, until the vegetables are just tender. Season to taste.

Sprinkle the chopped parsley into the pan. Stir in the smetana or crème fraîche and reheat gently. Serve hot.

Energy 361kcal/1503kJ; Protein 5.8g; Carbohydrate 31g, of which sugars 11.1g; Fat 24.7g, of which saturates 15.5g; Cholesterol 63mg; Calcium 94mg; Fibre 5.7g; Sodium 150mg.

SICILIAN MUSHROOM FRITTERS

These little fritters make a wonderful canapé or antipasto dish. They taste especially delicious when handed around with a cooling chopped cucumber and yogurt dip .

Makes 24

500g/1¼lb/8 cups mushrooms
2 eggs, beaten
3 garlic cloves, very finely
   chopped
45ml/3 tbsp chopped fresh
   parsley
45ml/3 tbsp grated Pecorino
   cheese
45ml/3 tbsp fresh white
   breadcrumbs
sunflower oil, for deep-frying
salt and ground black pepper

For the dip

½ cucumber, finely chopped
200ml/7fl oz/1 cup natural
   (plain) yogurt

To make the dip, combine the chopped cucumber and yogurt in a bowl and set aside.

Fill the base of a steamer with water and bring to the boil. Put the mushrooms in and steam until just cooked. Squeeze the mushrooms to remove some of the moisture and then chop them very finely in a food processor or with a heavy-bladed knife.

Put the chopped mushrooms in a bowl and add the eggs, garlic, parsley, cheese and breadcrumbs. Season and mix well.

Shape the mixture into 24 balls and flatten to make round fritters.

Heat the oil for deep-frying to 180°C/350°F or until a small piece of bread, dropped into the oil, browns in about 45 seconds. Fry the fritters, in batches if necessary, for 2–3 minutes until they rise to the surface and are crisp and golden.

Remove with a slotted spoon, drain on kitchen paper and keep hot while cooking successive batches. When all the fritters are cooked, serve them immediately with the cucumber and yogurt dip.

Energy 66kcal/274kJ; Protein 1.9g; Carbohydrate 1.6g, of which sugars 0.1g; Fat 5.9g, of which saturates 1.1g; Cholesterol 18mg; Calcium 33mg; Fibre 0.4g; Sodium 42mg.

PASTA, RICE AND PASTRIES

MUSHROOMS ADD THEIR DELICATE FLAVOUR TO

ALL SORTS OF PASTA, RICE AND PASTRY DISHES.

WITH THE ADDITION OF HERBS, NUTS, CHEESE,

BACON AND FRESH VEGETABLES, THEY ENHANCE

TARTS, RISOTTOS, STIR-FRIES AND SAUCES

WILD MUSHROOM AND FONTINA TART

Use any types of wild mushrooms you like in this tart – chanterelles, morels, and ceps all have wonderful flavours. It makes an impressive main course, served with a green salad.

Serves 6

*225g/8oz ready-made
   shortcrust pastry, thawed if
   frozen
50g/2oz/¼ cup butter
350g/12oz/4 cups mixed wild
   mushrooms, sliced if large
150g/5oz Fontina cheese, sliced
salt and ground black pepper*

Preheat the oven to 190°C/375°F/Gas 5. Roll out the pastry and use to line a 23cm/9in loose-bottomed flan tin (tart pan). Chill the pastry for 30 minutes, then bake blind for 15 minutes. Set aside.

Heat the butter in a large frying pan until foaming. Add the mushrooms and season with salt and ground black pepper. Cook over a medium heat for 4–5 minutes, moving the mushrooms about and turning them occasionally with a wooden spoon, until golden.

Arrange the mushrooms in the cooked pastry case with the Fontina cheese. Return the tart to the oven for 10 minutes, or until the cheese is golden and bubbling. Serve hot.

Energy 409kcal/1701kJ; Protein 10.2g; Carbohydrate 21.9g, of which sugars 2.3g; Fat 31g, of which saturates 13.4g; Cholesterol 143mg; Calcium 121mg; Fibre 2.3g; Sodium 199mg.

DUMPLINGS STUFFED WITH MUSHROOMS

Originally from Poland, these tiny stuffed dumplings are traditionally served as an accompaniment to borscht or clear soup, or as a light snack with a shot of vodka.

Serves 4–6

225g/8oz/2 cups plain (all-
    purpose) flour, plus extra for
    dusting
2.5ml/½ tsp salt
1 egg, beaten
30–45ml/2–3 tbsp lukewarm
    water
chopped fresh parsley, to
    garnish

For the filling

115g/4oz/2 cups dried
    mushrooms, rinsed and
    soaked in warm water for
    30 minutes
25g/1oz/2 tbsp butter
1 onion, very finely chopped
15ml/1 tbsp fresh white
    breadcrumbs
30ml/2 tbsp finely chopped
    fresh parsley
1 egg, beaten
salt and ground black pepper

To make the filling, drain the soaked mushrooms and chop very finely. Gently heat the butter in a large frying pan, add the onion and sauté for 5 minutes, or until softened.

Add the chopped mushrooms to the pan and cook for about 10 minutes, or until the liquid has evaporated and the mixture begins to sizzle in the pan.

Turn the mushroom mixture into a large bowl, then add the fresh white breadcrumbs, chopped parsley and egg. Season to taste and mix together to form a firm paste, then set aside and leave to cool slightly. (This mixture can be kept in the refrigerator for up to 24 hours.)

Sift the flour into a large bowl, mix in the salt, then make a dip in the middle with the back of a wooden spoon. Put the egg in the dip and stir in enough lukewarm water to form a stiff dough.

Turn the dough out on to a lightly floured surface and knead until pliant but fairly stiff. Leave to rest for 30 minutes. Roll out the dough thinly, to a thickness of about 3mm/⅛in, then cut into 5cm/2in squares.

Place a small amount of the mushroom filling in the centre of each square of dough. Fold one corner of the dough over the filling diagonally and press the edges together. Fold the two bottom corners of the triangle to the middle and press together to form a "pig's ear" shape.

Bring a large pan of lightly salted water to the boil. Drop in the dumplings and cook for about 3–5 minutes, or until they float to the surface. Lift out the dumplings with a slotted spoon and place on a warmed serving dish. Serve, garnished with chopped parsley.

Energy 198kcal/835kJ; Protein 6.4g; Carbohydrate 32g, of which sugars 1.3g; Fat 5.9g, of which saturates 2.8g; Cholesterol 72mg; Calcium 70mg; Fibre 1.5g; Sodium 70mg.

NOODLES WITH CRAB AND CLOUD EAR MUSHROOMS

This Vietnamese recipe is a dish of contrasting flavours, textures and colours resulting in a meal that will impress family and friends at a special celebratory dinner.

Serves 4

25g/1oz/¹/₂ cup dried cloud ear (wood ear) mushrooms, soaked in warm water for 20 minutes

115g/4oz dried bean thread (cellophane) noodles, soaked in warm water for 20 minutes

30ml/2 tbsp vegetable or sesame oil

3 shallots, halved and thinly sliced

2 garlic cloves, crushed

2 green or red Thai chillies, seeded and sliced

1 carrot, peeled and cut into thin diagonal rounds

5ml/1 tsp sugar

45ml/3 tbsp oyster sauce

15ml/1 tbsp soy sauce

400ml/14fl oz/1²/₃ cups water or chicken stock

225g/8oz fresh, raw crab meat, cut into bitesize chunks

ground black pepper

fresh coriander (cilantro) leaves, to garnish

Remove the centres from the soaked cloud ear mushrooms and cut the mushrooms in half. Drain the soaked noodles and cut them into 30cm/12in pieces.

Heat a wok or heavy pan and add 15ml/1 tbsp of the oil. Stir in the shallots, garlic and chillies, and cook until fragrant. Add the carrot rounds and cook for 1 minute, then add the mushrooms. Stir in the sugar with the oyster and soy sauces, followed by the bean thread noodles. Pour in the water or stock, cover the wok or pan and cook for 5 minutes, or until the noodles are soft and have absorbed most of the sauce.

Meanwhile, heat the remaining oil in a heavy pan. Add the crab meat and cook until it is nicely pink and tender. Season well with black pepper. Serve the noodles and crab meat, garnished with coriander.

Energy 292Kcal/1224kJ; Protein 16g; Carbohydrate 30g, of which sugars 5g; Fat 13g, of which saturates 2g; Cholesterol 36mg; Calcium 29mg; Fibre 2.5g; Sodium 1g

OVEN-BAKED PORCINI RISOTTO

This risotto is easy to make if you are pressed for time because you don't have to stand over it stirring constantly as it cooks, as you do with a traditional risotto.

Serves 4

25g/1oz/½ cup dried porcini mushrooms
750ml/1¼ pints/3 cups water
30ml/2 tbsp garlic-infused olive oil
1 onion, finely chopped
225g/8oz/generous 1 cup risotto rice
salt and ground black pepper

Put the mushrooms in a heatproof bowl and pour over 750ml/1¼ pints/3 cups boiling water. Leave to soak for 30 minutes. Drain the mushrooms through a sieve lined with kitchen paper, reserving the soaking liquor. Rinse the mushrooms thoroughly under running water to remove any grit, and dry on kitchen paper.

Preheat the oven to 180°C/350°F/Gas 4. Heat the oil in a roasting pan on the hob and add the onion. Cook for 2–3 minutes, or until softened but not coloured.

Add the rice and stir for 1–2 minutes, then add the mushrooms and stir. Pour in the mushroom liquor and mix well. Season with salt and pepper, and cover with foil.

Bake in the oven for 30 minutes, stirring occasionally, until all the stock has been absorbed and the rice is tender. Divide between warm serving bowls and serve immediately.

Energy 260kcal/1085kJ; Protein 4.8g;
Carbohydrate 46.2g, of which sugars 0.9g;
Fat 5.9g, of which saturates 0.8g;
Cholesterol 0mg; Calcium 16mg; Fibre
0.5g; Sodium 2mg.

BUCKWHEAT WITH CREAMED MUSHROOMS

Originally from Slovenia, this wholesome dish may be served alone with butter, buttermilk or yogurt, or with a root vegetable. It is unbeatable with wild mushrooms.

Serves 4

*250g/9oz/1¼ cups kasha
    (toasted buckwheat)*
*750ml/1¼ pints/3 cups
    vegetable stock*
75g/3oz/6 tbsp butter
1 onion, chopped
*500g/1¼lb/8 cups mixed wild
    and/or cultivated mushrooms*
*60ml/4 tbsp chopped fresh
    parsley, plus extra for
    garnishing*
250ml/8fl oz/1 cup sour cream
salt and ground black pepper

Put the kasha in a non-stick pan and toast over a medium heat, stirring for 3–4 minutes, until it has become slightly darker in colour. Turn down the heat to very low. Carefully pour over the stock, cover and simmer for 10–15 minutes, or until the kasha has absorbed all the stock and is tender.

Melt the butter in a frying pan. Add the onion and cook, stirring for 10 minutes until it is soft, but not browned. Add the mushrooms and cook, stirring frequently, until they are lightly browned in places and evenly cooked. The time will depend on the type, so be careful not to overcook any delicate mushrooms.

Add the parsley, cream and seasoning to the mushrooms, then heat for a few seconds. Add the kasha, fork the ingredients together lightly and serve at once, garnished with fresh parsley.

COOK'S TIP
Kasha is the name for whole buckwheat grains (often cracked) that have been roasted. Crushed and hulled unroasted buckwheat grains are used in porridge.

Energy 436kcal/1808kJ; Protein 8.4g; Carbohydrate 36.7g, of which sugars 3.9g; Fat 29.3g, of which saturates 17.7g; Cholesterol 77mg; Calcium 115mg; Fibre 2.3g; Sodium 151mg.

BUCKWHEAT, MUSHROOM AND PASTA

This combination of buckwheat, mushrooms and bow-shaped pasta is heavenly. To people who have not been raised on buckwheat it may taste grainy but once tried, it will be never forgotten.

Serves 4–6

25g/1oz/½ cup dried well-
   flavoured mushrooms, such
   as ceps
500ml/17fl oz/2¼ cups boiling
   stock or water
45ml/3 tbsp rendered chicken
   fat (for a meat meal),
   vegetable oil (for a
   vegetarian meal)
3–4 onions, thinly sliced
250g/9oz/3 cups mushrooms,
   sliced
300g/11oz/1½ cups whole,
   coarse, medium or fine
   buckwheat
200g/7oz pasta bows
salt and ground black pepper

Put the dried mushrooms in a bowl, pour over half the boiling stock or water and leave to stand for 20–30 minutes, until reconstituted. Remove the mushrooms from the liquid, then strain and reserve the liquid.

Heat the chicken fat, or oil in a frying pan, add the onions and fry for 5–10 minutes until softened and beginning to brown. Remove the onions to a plate, then add the sliced mushrooms to the pan and fry briefly. Add the soaked mushrooms and cook for 2–3 minutes. Return the onions to the pan and set aside.

Stir the remaining boiling stock and the reserved mushroom liquid into the buckwheat, cover the pan, and cook for about 10 minutes until the buckwheat is just tender and all of the liquid has been absorbed.

Meanwhile, cook the pasta in a large pan of salted boiling water as directed on the packet, or until just tender, then drain.

When the kasha is cooked, toss in the onions and mushrooms, and the pasta. Season and serve hot.

Energy 364kcal/1529kJ; Protein 10.3g;
Carbohydrate 67g, of which sugars 4g; Fat
7.3g, of which saturates 3.6g; Cholesterol
14mg; Calcium 47mg; Fibre 2.2g; Sodium
48mg.

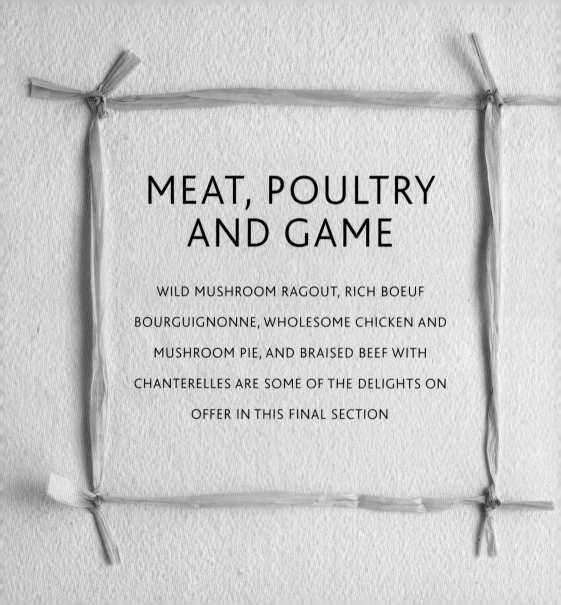

MEAT, POULTRY AND GAME

WILD MUSHROOM RAGOUT, RICH BOEUF
BOURGUIGNONNE, WHOLESOME CHICKEN AND
MUSHROOM PIE, AND BRAISED BEEF WITH
CHANTERELLES ARE SOME OF THE DELIGHTS ON
OFFER IN THIS FINAL SECTION

ROE DEER CUTLETS WITH MUSHROOMS

Venison is a classic Scandinavian dish and roe deer is particularly tender. Accompanied by sautéed mushrooms in a rich, creamy sauce it is a dish worth savouring.

Serves 6

75g/3oz/6 tbsp butter

200g/7oz/2½ cups chanterelle (girolle) mushrooms, halved if large

200g/7oz/2½ cups trumpet mushrooms

2kg/4½lb saddle of roe deer (12 cutlets), trimmed by the butcher

1 litre/1¾ pints/4 cups water

3 shallots, chopped

5 juniper berries, crushed

1 fresh thyme sprig, chopped

1 bay leaf

225g/8oz potatoes, cut into 5mm/¼in cubes

6 small carrots, cut into 5mm/¼in cubes

120ml/4fl oz/½ cup double (heavy) cream

salt and ground black pepper

Energy 455kcal/1903kJ; Protein 40.7g; Carbohydrate 19.3g, of which sugars 6.8g; Fat 25.4g, of which saturates 14.7g; Cholesterol 137mg; Calcium 50mg; Fibre 3g; Sodium 193mg.

In a large frying pan, melt 25g/1oz/2 tbsp of the butter, add all the mushrooms and sauté until browned. Meanwhile, season the cutlets with salt and pepper. Melt 25g/1oz/2 tbsp of the butter in a flameproof casserole, add the cutlets and fry for 2–3 minutes until browned.

Add the water, shallots, juniper berries, thyme and bay leaf to the cutlets. Bring to the boil then simmer for 10 minutes to reduce the liquid.

Meanwhile, melt half the remaining butter in a large frying pan. Add the potatoes and fry for about 20 minutes, stirring occasionally, until golden brown. Transfer to a serving dish and keep warm. Fry the carrots in the remaining butter until golden.

Add the cream to the casserole and continue to cook for 20 minutes. Finally, add the sautéed mushrooms. Serve hot, with the fried potatoes and carrots.

BOEUF BOURGUIGNONNE

The classic French dish of beef cooked in Burgundy style, with red wine, small pieces of bacon, baby onions and mushrooms, is cooked for several hours at a low temperature.

Serves 6

175g/6oz rindless streaky (fatty) bacon rashers, chopped
900g/2lb lean braising steak
30ml/2 tbsp plain (all-purpose) flour
45ml/3 tbsp sunflower oil
25g/1oz/2 tbsp butter
12 shallots, peeled and left whole
2 garlic cloves, crushed
175g/6oz/2 cups mushrooms, sliced
450ml/¾ pint/scant 2 cups robust red wine
150ml/¼ pint/⅔ cup beef stock
1 bay leaf
2 sprigs each of fresh thyme, parsley and marjoram
salt and ground black pepper
mashed root vegetables, to serve

Energy 749kcal/3117kJ; Protein 63.3g;
Carbohydrate 15.2g, of which sugars 8.8g;
Fat 40.3g, of which saturates 14g;
Cholesterol 167mg; Calcium 69mg; Fibre
2.8g; Sodium 868mg.

Preheat the oven to 160°C/325°F/Gas 3. Heat a large flameproof casserole, then add the bacon and cook, stirring occasionally, until the pieces are crisp and golden brown.

Meanwhile, cut the meat into 2.5cm/1in cubes. Season the flour and use to coat the meat. Use a draining spoon to remove the bacon from the casserole and set aside. Heat the oil, then brown the beef in batches and set aside with the bacon.

Add the butter to the fat remaining in the casserole. Cook the shallots and garlic until just starting to colour, then add the mushrooms and cook for a further 5 minutes. Replace the bacon and meat, and stir in the wine and stock. Tie the bay leaf, thyme, parsley and marjoram together into a bouquet garni and add to the casserole.

Cover and cook in the oven for 1½ hours, or until the meat is tender, stirring once or twice. Season to taste and serve the casserole with creamy mashed root vegetables, such as celeriac and potatoes.

BEEF WITH CHANTERELLE MUSHROOMS

Use really good beef and rapidly fry the dried pieces quickly so the outside is well browned and the inside very rare. Chanterelle (girolle) mushrooms are the best mushrooms for this recipe.

Serves 4

115g/4oz/1½ cups chanterelle
   (girolle) mushrooms
2 rump (round) steaks,
   175g/6oz each, cut into strips
45ml/3 tbsp olive oil
1 garlic clove, crushed
1 shallot, finely chopped
60ml/4 tbsp dry white wine
60ml/4 tbsp double (heavy)
   cream
25g/1oz/2 tbsp butter
salt and ground black pepper
chopped fresh watercress, to
   garnish

Clean the mushrooms. If you have collected them from the wild cut off the ends where they have come from the ground and, using kitchen paper, wipe off any leaf matter or moss that may be adhering to them. Cut the mushrooms in half through the stalk and cap.

Dry the beef thoroughly on kitchen paper. Heat a large frying pan over a high heat then add 30ml/2 tbsp olive oil. Working in batches (see Cook's Tip) put the meat in the pan and quickly brown on all sides.

Remove the meat, which should still be very rare, from the pan, set aside and keep warm. Add the remaining olive oil to the pan and reduce the heat. Stir in the garlic and shallot and cook, stirring, for about 1 minute. Then increase the heat and add the mushrooms. Season and cook until the mushrooms just start to soften. Add the wine, bring to the boil and add the cream. As the liquid thickens, return the beef to the pan and heat through.

Remove the pan from the heat and swirl in the butter without mixing fully. Serve on warmed plates, garnished with chopped fresh watercress.

Energy 415kcal/1725kJ; Protein 29.9g; Carbohydrate 0.7g, of which sugars 0.6g; Fat 31g, of which saturates 14.2g; Cholesterol 122mg; Calcium 21mg; Fibre 0.4g; Sodium 124mg.

COOK'S TIP
• When browning meat in a hot pan don't put too much in at once as this lowers the temperature too quickly and the meat will poach instead of fry. Put in a few pieces at first, then wait 10–15 seconds before adding more.

MARINATED MUSHROOMS WITH HAM

This dish is usually served cold but tastes equally good hot from the pan. Use as many varieties of mushrooms as you like to make the most of their various flavours and textures.

Serves 4

400g/14oz/5 cups mixed
   mushrooms, such as chestnut
   (cremini) and oyster
   mushrooms
30ml/2 tbsp olive oil
200g/7oz raw ham, sausages
   and bacon, diced
2 garlic cloves, finely chopped
15–30ml/1–2 tbsp white wine
   vinegar
45ml/3 tbsp chopped fresh
   parsley

Wipe the mushrooms clean and cut or tear the larger ones in half or into quarters.

Heat the olive oil in a frying pan. Add the meat and cook over a low heat, stirring frequently, for about 5 minutes.

Add the mushrooms, increase the heat to high and cook, stirring constantly, for 5 minutes. Add the garlic and 15ml/1 tbsp of the vinegar and cook for 1 minute more.

Remove the pan from the heat and stir in the parsley. Serve immediately or, if you want to serve the mushrooms cold, add the remaining vinegar and leave to cool.

Energy 130kcal/541kJ; Protein 12.1g; Carbohydrate 3.1g, of which sugars 1g; Fat 7.8g, of which saturates 1.5g; Cholesterol 29mg; Calcium 20mg; Fibre 1.8g; Sodium 607mg.

VARIATION

When served hot, these mushrooms also go well with scrambled eggs.

CHICKEN AND MUSHROOM PIE

Chicken pie is a perfect meal for either a mid-week supper or Sunday lunch. If you can find them, use wild mushrooms to intensify the flavours.

Serves 6

50g/2oz/¼ cup butter
30ml/2 tbsp plain (all-purpose) flour
250ml/8fl oz/1 cup hot chicken stock
60ml/4 tbsp single (light) cream
1 onion, coarsely chopped
2 carrots, sliced
2 celery sticks, chopped
50g/2oz/¾ cup fresh mushrooms
450g/1lb/2 cups cooked chicken meat, cubed
50g/2oz/½ cup peas
salt and ground black pepper
beaten egg, to glaze

For the pastry

225g/8oz/2 cups plain (all-purpose) flour
1.5ml/¼ tsp salt
115g/4oz/½ cup cold butter, diced
65g/2½oz/⅓ cup white vegetable fat (shortening), diced
120ml/8 tbsp chilled water

To make the pastry, sift the flour and salt into a bowl. Rub in the butter and white vegetable fat until the mixture resembles breadcrumbs. Sprinkle with 90ml/6 tbsp chilled water and mix until the dough holds together. If the dough is too crumbly, add a little more water.

Gather the dough into a ball and flatten it into a round. Wrap in clear film (plastic wrap) and chill in the refrigerator for at least 30 minutes.

Preheat the oven to 190°C/375°F/Gas 5. To make the filling, melt half the butter over a low heat. Whisk in the flour and cook until bubbling, whisking constantly. Add the hot stock and whisk over a medium heat until the mixture boils. Cook for 2–3 minutes, then whisk in the cream. Season to taste, and set aside.

Heat the remaining butter in a large non-stick frying pan and cook the onion and carrots over a low heat for about 5 minutes. Add the celery and mushrooms and cook for a further 5 minutes, until they have softened. Add the cooked chicken and peas and stir in thoroughly.

Add the chicken mixture to the sauce. Spoon the mixture into a 2.5 litre/4 pint/2½ quart oval baking dish.

Roll out the pastry on a floured surface to a thickness of about 3mm/⅛in. Cut out an oval 2.5cm/1in larger all around than the dish. Lay the pastry over the filling. Gently press around the edge of the dish to seal, then trim off the excess pastry. Crimp the edge of the pastry by pinching it between forefinger and thumb. Continue all round the pastry edge. Glaze the lid with beaten egg and cut several slits in the pastry to allow the steam to escape. Bake the pie in the preheated oven for about 30 minutes, until the pastry has browned. Serve hot.

Energy 600kcal/2501kJ; Protein 23.7g; Carbohydrate 38.8g, of which sugars 3.7g; Fat 40g, of which saturates 21.8g; Cholesterol 132mg; Calcium 92mg; Fibre 2.7g; Sodium 226mg.

CHICKEN BREASTS STUFFED WITH WILD MUSHROOMS

Here wild mushrooms are combined with juniper berries and minced (ground) veal or chicken to make a richly flavoured stuffing for chicken breast fillets.

Serves 4

4 skinless chicken breast fillets, about 150g/5¼oz each
45ml/3 tbsp vegetable oil
10g/¼oz/½ tbsp butter
300g/11oz/4 cups wild mushrooms, chopped
6 juniper berries, crushed
1 shallot, grated
115g/4oz/½ cup minced (ground) veal or chicken
1 egg, beaten
60ml/4 tbsp chopped fresh parsley
15ml/1 tbsp chopped fresh dill
30ml/2 tbsp chopped fresh thyme
8 streaky (fatty) bacon rashers
100ml/3½fl oz/scant ½ cup chicken stock
100ml/3½fl oz/scant ½ cup white wine
30ml/2 tbsp sour cream
30ml/2 tbsp creamed horseradish
salt and ground black pepper
spinach leaves, to serve

Preheat the oven to 180°C/350°F/Gas 4. Put each chicken breast fillet on a board, cover with clear film (plastic wrap) and pound with a meat pounder or a rolling pin until thinned and enlarged. This will make it large enough to stuff easily.

Put half the oil and all the butter in a large frying pan and add the mushrooms, then sauté for 5–6 minutes, or until wilted and cooked. Transfer into a bowl and add the juniper berries, shallot, minced veal or chicken, egg and herbs. Combine well and season to taste.

Divide the filling among the chicken fillets and roll them up to enclose. Wrap each with two bacon rashers.

Heat the remaining oil in a heavy frying pan that can be used in the oven, or a flameproof casserole, over medium-high heat, and add the chicken fillets with the bacon seams down. Cook, turning, to brown the rolls all over, pressing gently at first to seal. Add the stock and white wine, then put the pan in the oven and cook for 30 minutes, or until the chicken is cooked through.

Remove the chicken rolls from the pan and leave to rest on a warm serving plate. Put the pan on the stove over a medium heat and simmer to reduce the cooking liquid. Add the sour cream and horseradish, then heat through. Serve the chicken with the sauce, accompanied by steamed spinach leaves.

Energy 456kcal/1902kJ; Protein 47.3g; Carbohydrate 2.5g, of which sugars 2.1g; Fat 26.9g, of which saturates 7.8g; Cholesterol 154mg; Calcium 74mg; Fibre 1.8g; Sodium 608mg.

PHEASANT AND WILD MUSHROOM RAGOÛT

Game birds and wild mushrooms make wonderful culinary partners. This traditional dish from the Scottish Highlands brings out the best in both of them.

Serves 4

4 pheasant breasts, skinned
vegetable oil, for braising
12 shallots, halved
2 garlic cloves, crushed
75g/3oz/1 cup wild
  mushrooms, sliced
75ml/2½fl oz/⅓ cup port
150ml/¼ pint/⅔ cup chicken
  stock
sprigs of fresh parsley and
  thyme
1 bay leaf
grated rind (zest) of 1 lemon
200ml/7fl oz/scant 1 cup

COOK'S TIP
This dish is delicious served with pilau rice.

Dice and season the pheasant breasts. Heat a little oil in a heavy pan and colour the pheasant meat quickly. Remove the meat from the pan and set aside.

Add the shallots to the pan, fry quickly to colour a little then add the garlic and sliced mushrooms. Reduce the heat and cook gently for 5 minutes.

Pour the port and stock into the pan and add the herbs, lemon rind and season. Reduce a little. When the shallots are nearly cooked add the cream, reduce to thicken then return the meat. Allow to cook for a few minutes before serving.

Energy 530kcal/2200kJ; Protein 34.1g; Carbohydrate 7.4g, of which sugars 5.9g; Fat 33g, of which saturates 20.2g; Cholesterol 69mg; Calcium 91mg; Fibre 1.1g; Sodium 114mg.

INDEX

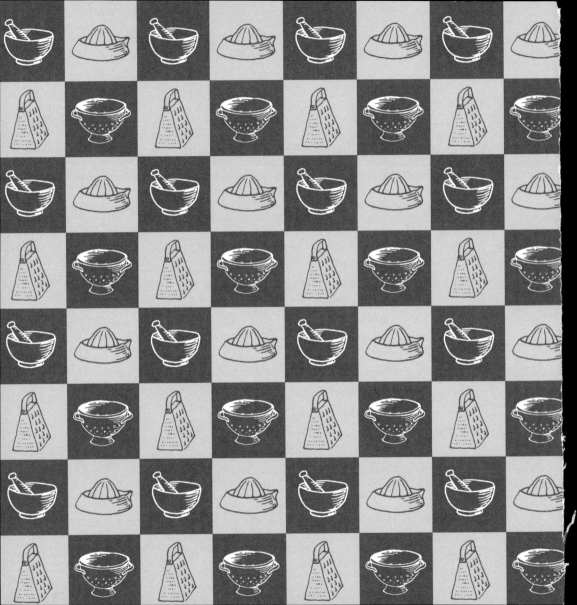